WITHDRAWN

EDGE
BOOKS

GOLDEN RETRIEVERS

By Brekka Hervey Larrew

Consultant: Sandi Haessler
Central Region Director
Golden Retriever Club of America

Capstone
press

Mankato, Minnesota

Edge Books are published by Capstone Press,
151 Good Counsel Drive, P.O. Box 669, Mankato, Minnesota 56002.
www.capstonepress.com

Library of Congress Cataloging-in-Publication Data
Larrew, Brekka Hervey.
    Golden retrievers / by Brekka Hervey Larrew.
    p. cm. — (Edge books. All about dogs)
    Includes bibliographical references and index.
    ISBN-13: 978-1-4296-1949-3 (hardcover)
    ISBN-10: 1-4296-1949-X (hardcover)
    1. Golden retriever — Juvenile literature. I. Title. II. Series.
SF429.G63L37 2009
636.752'7 — dc22   2008001231

Summary: Describes the history, physical features, temperament, and care of the
    golden retriever breed.

Editorial Credits
Erika L. Shores, editor; Veronica Bianchini, designer; Marcie Spence,
    photo researcher

Photo Credits
Capstone Press/Karon Dubke, cover, 1, 12 (bottom), 16 (top and bottom right),
    18, 19, 22, 25, 27, 28, 29, 30
Courtesy of the Golden Retriever Club of America, 11 (both), 12 (top)
Dreamstime/Tomislav Birtic, 17; Volcomstone14bw, 26
fotolia/EastWest Imaging, 23; timur1970, 9
Getty Images Inc./Joseph H. Bailey/National Geographic, 6–7
iStockphoto/Sue McDonald, 24
Peter Arnold/O. Diez, 15
Photo by Fiona Green, 5, 16 (bottom left)
Shutterstock/iofoto, 20; pixshots, 14; Tommy Maenhout, 16 (middle)

**Capstone Press thanks Martha Diedrich, dog trainer, for her assistance
    with this book.**

Table of Contents

CHAPTER 1

A PERFECT DOG

In the 1800s, one of England's wealthiest citizens decided to breed the perfect hunting dog. The golden retriever was created as a result of this quest.

In many dog lovers' eyes, golden retrievers are indeed perfect. Their fans believe they are beautiful. They are playful, easy to housebreak, and are among the most **obedient** dog breeds in the world. Hunters love how their loyal companions follow a trail and retrieve the birds they have shot. People with disabilities appreciate golden retrievers as hardworking, loyal service dogs. Golden retrievers, sometimes called goldens, do have one imperfection, though. They are too friendly for guard duty!

obedient — able to follow rules and commands

Many people can't resist the friendly face of the golden retriever.

Golden retriever puppies stay with their mothers for at least seven weeks.

Golden retriever fans especially appreciate the breed's boundless energy. Goldens can enjoy a long game of fetch with their owners.

Despite their high energy, goldens are gentle. Small children sometimes play roughly with animals. Goldens will often tolerate children tugging on their ears and tails.

Finding a Golden

Does a friendly family dog sound right for you? If so, it's not the best idea to rush into finding a puppy. Finding the right puppy takes time and patience. First, find a **breeder** whose goal is to produce healthy golden retriever puppies with pleasant personalities. Good breeders register with the American Kennel Club (AKC).

After selecting a breeder, it is important to visit a litter and look at the puppies' parents. The puppy will probably look and act like its parents when it's older.

breeder — someone who breeds and raises dogs or other animals

Some people who want a dog are not interested in training a puppy. Others wish to give a home to a needy adult golden retriever. Adult dogs often have a difficult time finding homes because many people wish to raise puppies. To find an adult golden, people can contact animal shelters, a rescue organization, or even a breeder. Sometimes people who can no longer care for their dogs return them to the breeder.

EDGE FACT

In 2006, nearly 43,000 golden retrievers were registered with the AKC. It was the fourth most popular breed in the country.

Sometimes older dogs end up in shelters if their owners can no longer care for them.

CHAPTER 2

HISTORY OF GOLDENS

For nearly 100 years, many historical books told a story about golden retrievers that was wrong. According to the myth, a Scottish **aristocrat** named Lord Tweedmouth purchased some Russian circus dogs. These circus dogs were the first golden retrievers.

Over the years, people traveled to Russia to find similar dogs that they could mate with the descendants of Tweedmouth's dogs. They had no luck finding any because Tweedmouth's dogs did not come from Russia after all.

In the 1950s, two golden retriever fans discovered the real story of Lord Tweedmouth's dogs. Elma Stonex and the sixth Earl of Illchester studied Tweedmouth's breeding records. They discovered that he never bought dogs from a Russian circus. However, he did buy a yellow retriever named Nous from a man in Brighton, England. Nous and a liver-colored spaniel named Belle were mated. Their four yellow puppies, born in 1868, were the beginning of today's golden retrievers.

aristocrat — a member of the highest social rank

Nous was a yellow retriever used to start the golden retriever breed.

The spaniel in this painting looks much like the one mated with Nous.

Lord Tweedmouth was also known as Sir Dudley Majoriebanks. His search for the perfect hunting dog led to the golden retriever breed.

After these four puppies were born, Lord Tweedmouth mated some of his dogs with other breeds. The other breeds had traits he wanted to strengthen in his new breed. For example, he bred wavy and flat-coated retrievers with his dogs to ensure a strong retrieving instinct. This instinct causes a dog to retrieve a fallen bird rather than to eat it where it is found. He even used a sandy-colored bloodhound to improve his breed's ability to identify and follow scents.

A Golden Age

Tweedmouth's new breed was also popular outside of Europe. By the early 1890s, owners were bringing golden retrievers across the Atlantic Ocean to Canada and the United States.

By the 1930s, people throughout the United States were becoming fans of goldens. The American Kennel Club registered the first golden retriever in 1925. Owners soon began entering their golden retrievers in dog shows.

Today, the golden retriever enjoys enormous popularity. It is among the most popular breeds in North America, Europe, and Australia.

CHAPTER 3

GOLDEN HAIR

The golden retriever is named for its most distinguishing feature — its coat. Coat shades can range from a light champagne cream to a deep golden red. Goldens have two types of hair in their coats — a topcoat and an undercoat. The water-resistant topcoat is straight or slightly wavy. The topcoat sheds in small amounts throughout the year. The soft undercoat keeps the dog cool in summer and warm in winter. The undercoat sheds in spring and fall.

Golden retrievers are medium-sized dogs. They stand 21.5 to 24 inches (55 to 61 centimeters) tall at the shoulders. They weigh between 55 and 75 pounds (25 and 34 kilograms).

A golden retriever's muscular body is built for hunting. They can swim through cold water to retrieve water birds. Hunting also requires great endurance. Goldens have a lot of energy for running, working, and playing.

A golden retriever's coat is suited for spending time in the water.

Everything about a golden's face gives it a friendly appearance. The dog seems to smile. Its brown eyes look alert and intelligent. A golden has short, hanging ears and a medium-length muzzle. Its black nose has a keen sense of smell.

The tail of a golden retriever is thick at the base and narrow at the tip. The tail is feathery underneath. It is very soft, but it is also very strong. It acts like a rudder to help steer the dog while swimming.

Like all dogs, goldens wag their long, straight tails when they are happy or excited.

EDGE FACT

Golden retrievers belong to a group of dogs called "gun dogs." Bird hunters use these dogs to retrieve dead birds. Today, however, most goldens are raised purely to be pets.

A Quick Learner

Golden retrievers are quick learners and love to please their owners. Goldens can easily learn to be housebroken and trained to walk on a leash. Goldens also enjoy learning tricks. When a golden learns a new skill, owners often give a treat or a pat on the head. This praise and affection, and a little bit of practice, are all it takes for a golden to learn.

Many people think goldens are the easiest breed of dog to train.

People in wheelchairs train their goldens to retrieve all sorts of items for them.

Because goldens are so trainable, they are often used for important work. They are a popular guide dog for people who are blind. People who need wheelchairs rely on their goldens to retrieve items that are out of reach.

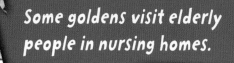
Some goldens visit elderly people in nursing homes.

In addition, the police and military use goldens to sniff for drugs or bombs at airports and international borders. Goldens also help rescue people after earthquakes and other natural disasters. Studies show that their noses can even detect some types of cancer.

Friendly Dogs

Golden retrievers are easygoing and friendly. They enjoy being with their owners and often follow them from room to room. They are even likely to make friends with the neighborhood cats. They tolerate children well, which makes them a popular choice for a family dog. Their sweet nature also makes them well suited for work as therapy dogs. Goldens used as therapy dogs visit patients who are receiving long-term hospital care or elderly patients in nursing homes.

EDGE FACT

Golden retrievers have saved lives. They have saved their owners from wild animals such as bears, coyotes, and mountain lions. Other goldens have awakened their owners when their homes were on fire.

CHAPTER 4

CARING FOR A GOLDEN

Caring for a golden retriever goes beyond just feeding and walking it. Training a golden is an important step in giving it a happy life.

A well-mannered pet is much more fun than a disobedient one. Many golden owners take their puppies to obedience classes to encourage good manners. In these classes, dogs learn to follow simple commands. One important command to learn is "sit." If a dog sits before being petted, it's less likely to jump on people when first meeting them. Teaching a dog to come when called keeps it safe.

Obedience classes often teach the owners about caring for their dogs, too. The classes encourage a healthy relationship between the owner and the dog.

Rewarding a golden with a treat helps it learn new commands.

Playful goldens love to use their retrieving skills in a game of fetch.

As with any dog, a golden needs to learn the rules for living in its owner's house. Everyone in the family must be consistent in enforcing the rules. Otherwise, the dog will become confused. When a dog is successful in following the rules, rewards encourage it to repeat the good behavior. The best rewards include dog treats, praise, and affection.

In addition to commands, goldens enjoy learning games. Because they were bred for retrieving, a simple game of fetch can last for hours. One game that takes advantage of the breed's great sense of smell is hide-and-seek. In this game, the golden locates a hidden object by sniffing for it.

Feeding, Grooming, and Veterinary Care

Goldens love to eat, but they shouldn't be overfed.
Obesity is common in the breed and causes health problems.
Puppies should eat about 3 cups (720 mL) of food per day.
Adult dogs should eat 3 to 5 cups (720 mL to 1,200 mL)
per day depending on the food and how active the dog is.
All dogs need water available to them at all times.

Active puppies need plenty of water to drink.

Because goldens have a lot of hair, grooming is
important. Goldens need a bath about every two months.
They also require weekly brushing. Frequent brushing
can help reduce shedding.

Ears and nails also need attention. Dirty ears are more
likely to become infected than clean ears. Overgrown nails
can hurt the dog and scratch an owner's skin or furniture.

All dogs need veterinary care. Goldens must have a yearly checkup where they receive any necessary **vaccinations**. Many owners choose to have a veterinarian spay or neuter their dog. This surgery prevents certain cancers, and may help the dog live a longer life. Spaying and neutering also helps control the pet population by preventing unwanted puppies from being born.

The Perfect Friend

Golden retrievers usually live 10 to 12 years. Their long life span means owning one is a long-term commitment. Golden owners have the opportunity for a long and happy relationship with their pet. Bred as the perfect hunting dog, goldens make perfect friends for thousands of dog owners throughout the world.

vaccination — a shot of medicine that protects animals from a disease

Loyal golden retrievers love to spend time with their owners.

Glossary

aristocrat (uh-RIS-tuh-krat) — a member of a group of people thought to be the best in some way, usually based on how much money they have; aristocrats are members of the highest social rank or nobility.

breed (BREED) — a certain kind of animal within an animal group; breed also means to mate and raise a certain kind of animal.

breeder (BREE-duhr) — someone who breeds and raises dogs or other animals

descendant (di-SEN-duhnt) — a dog's offspring and family members born to those offspring

obedient (oh-BEE-dee-uhnt) — able to follow rules and commands

obesity (oh-BEE-suh-tee) — to be extremely overweight

vaccination (vak-suh-NAY-shun) — a shot of medicine that protects animals from a disease

Read More

Gray, Susan H. *Golden Retrievers*. Domestic Dogs. Chanhassen, Minn.: Child's World, 2007.

Morn, September. *The Golden Retriever*. Our Best Friends. Pittsburgh: ElDorado Ink, 2008.

Internet Sites

FactHound offers a safe, fun way to find Internet sites related to this book. All of the sites on FactHound have been researched by our staff.

Here's how:

1. Visit *www.facthound.com*
2. Choose your grade level.
3. Type in this book ID **142961949X** for age-appropriate sites. You may also browse subjects by clicking on letters, or by clicking on pictures and words.
4. Click on the **Fetch It** button.

FactHound will fetch the best sites for you!

Index